The Story of Coding

By James Floyd Kelly

US Senior Editor Shannon Beatty
Senior Editor Caryn Jenner
Editor Radhika Haswani
Project Art Editor Yamini Panwar
Art Editors Emma Hobson, Kanika Kalra, Rashika Kachroo
Jacket Editor Francesca Young
Jacket Designers Dheeraj Arora, Amy Keast
DTP Designer Dheeraj Singh
Sr. DTP Designer Jagtar Singh
Picture Researcher Sakshi Saluja
Producer, Pre-Production Nadine King
Producer Niamh Tierney
Managing Editor Laura Gilbert
Deputy Managing Editor Vineetha Mokkil
Managing Art Editors Neha Ahuja Chowdhry, Diane Peyton Jones
Art Director Martin Wilson
Publisher Sarah Larter

First American Edition, 2017
Published in the United States by DK Publishing
345 Hudson Street, New York, New York 10014

Copyright © 2017 Dorling Kindersley Limited
DK, a Penguin Random House Company
17 18 19 20 21 10 9 8 7 6 5 4 3 2 1
001—305119—Jun/17

A CIP catalogue record for this book is available from the British Library.

ISBN: 978-1-4654-6242-8 (Paperback)
ISBN: 978-1-4654-6231-2 (Hardcover)

Printed and bound in China.

The publisher would like to thank the following for their kind permission to reproduce their photographs:
(Key: a-above; b-below/bottom; c-center; f-far; l-left; r-right; t-top)
1 Dreamstime.com: Boris Zatserkovnyy. **4 123RF.com**: scanrail (b). **6 Dreamstime.com**: Sashkinw (b). **7 Dreamstime.com**: Vera
Volkova. **8 123RF.com**: backgroundstore (b). **10 123RF.com**: cobalt (b); wojciech kaczkowski (ca). **11 Dreamstime.com**: Anton
Samsonov / iPod is a trademark of Apple Inc., registered in the U.S. and other countries (t); hxdyl (b). **12 Dorling Kindersley**: The
Science Museum, London (br). **13 Alamy Stock Photo**: Soberka Richard / Hemis.fr (t). John McLinden: (br). **14 Alamy Stock Photo**:
IanDagnall Computing (cra); Photo Researchers (tl). **15 Getty Images**: Science & Society Picture Library (cb). **16 Alamy Stock
Photo**: INTERFOTO (tl). **17 Science Photo Library**: James King-Holmes / Bletchley Park Trust. **18–19 Getty Images**: Historical (b).
19 Alamy Stock Photo: Marek Kosmal (cr). **20 Science Photo Library**: Earl Scott (b). **21 123RF.com**: Maxim Basinski (bl).
Alamy Stock Photo: B Christopher (tc). **Getty Images**: Science & Society Picture Library (cr). **22 Dreamstime.com**: Darkworx (br).
23 Alamy Stock Photo: Stefan Sollfors (cl). **Dreamstime.com**: Maciek905 (bl). **25 Alamy Stock Photo**: Erik Tham (c). **31 123RF.
com**: Wavebreak Media Ltd (cb). **Alamy Stock Photo**: MIKA Images (t). **32–33 Dreamstime.com**: Wavebreakmedia (b).
37 Alamy Stock Photo: Stephen Lam (br). **38–39 Getty Images**: Andrew Burton (b)

Jacket images: Front: 123RF.com: Andrey KOTKO, scanrail cb

All other images © Dorling Kindersley
For further information see: www.dkimages.com

Contents

Words in **bold** appear in the glossary.

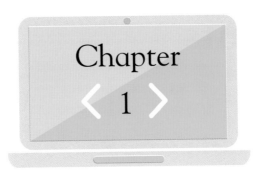

Chapter 1

What is Coding?

The modern world is full of computers! There are desktops, laptops, and tablets. Even a cell phone is a mini computer.

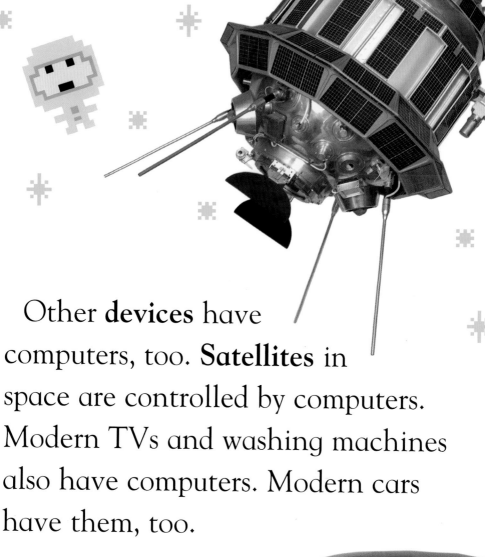

Other **devices** have computers, too. **Satellites** in space are controlled by computers. Modern TVs and washing machines also have computers. Modern cars have them, too.

The parts of a device that you can touch are called hardware. The program that tells a computer what to do is software. Hardware and software work together.

For example, an elevator is hardware. Press the button for your floor, and the software program tells the elevator where to go.

Computer programs are called code. Code is a set of instructions for a computer to follow.

```
▶ <head>...</head>
▼ <body class=" customize-support">
  ▼ <div class="wrapper">
    ▶ <header>...</header>
    ▶ <div id="loading-zone" class>...</div>
    ▶ <div id="content" class="mod centered homepa
    ▶ <div id="landscape-image-magnifier" style="d
    ▶ <div id="landscape-image-magnifier" style="di
      <div class="push"></div>
  </div>
  ▶ <footer class="footer">...</footer>
    <script type="text/javascript"> Cufon.now(); </s
    <script type="text/javascript" src="http://backg
  ▶ <script type="text/javascript">...</script>
  ▶ <div id="wpadminbar" class role="navigation">...</d
</body>
html>
```

Code on a computer screen

Coding is writing step-by-step instructions for a computer. For example, here are instructions for an elevator.

1. Wait for doors to close.

2. Wait for button to be pressed.

If button pressed is higher than current floor, move upward.

If button pressed is lower than current floor, move downward.

3. When current floor is the same as button pressed, open doors.

Computers Everywhere

Computer coding is used for many different things.

Global Positioning Systems (GPS)

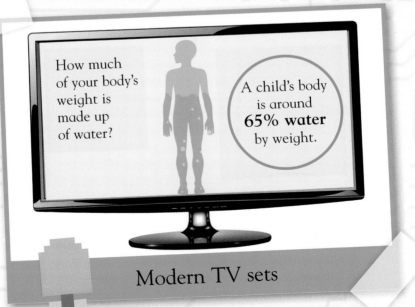

How much of your body's weight is made up of water?

A child's body is around **65% water** by weight.

Modern TV sets

Making books

Airplane controls

Early Computers

The abacus is sometimes called the first computer. It was invented more than 2,000 years ago to help with math.

Old Chinese abacus

The loom weaves a pattern shown
by a punch card.

A loom weaves thread into cloth.
In 1801, French weaver Joseph
Jacquard made punch cards with
holes for his loom. The holes told
the loom how to weave patterns in
the cloth. These holes were an
early computer code.

Punch card

Ada Lovelace

In the mid-1800s, Charles Babbage invented the Analytical Engine to do math problems. His friend, Ada Lovelace, wrote step-by-step programs for the Analytical Engine.

She is known as the world's first computer programmer. Lovelace realized that computers could do lots of different **tasks**.

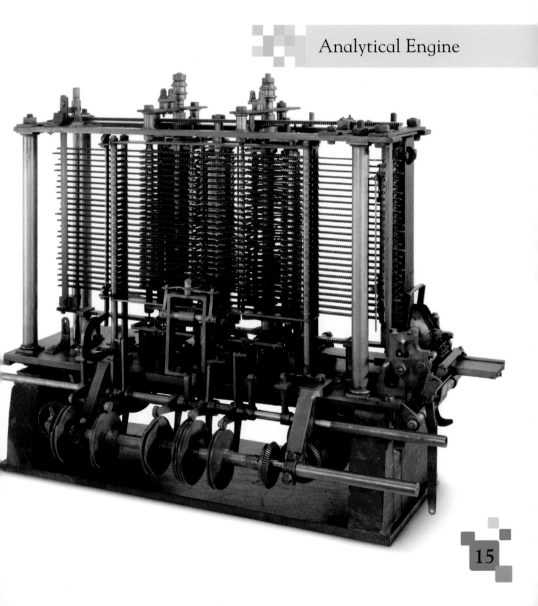

Analytical Engine

Enigma coding machine

During World War II (1939–1945), German forces used a secret code called Enigma. Countries fighting against Germany needed to crack the Enigma code to get important information. British scientist Alan Turing invented a computer that decoded Enigma and helped to end the war.

Turing's computer was called the Bombe.

ENIAC was the first computer that could be programmed to do different tasks. ENIAC was so big, it took up the space of a whole room!

Operators programmed ENIAC by putting plugs into large boards.

Since then, computers have become smaller and smaller. Now, small devices such as cell phones use tiny **computer chips**.

Modern computer chip

Past and Present

See how computers have changed!

FACT!

In 1947, a moth trapped in a computer caused the computer to make mistakes. It was the first computer bug!

1960s

1970s

ALTAIR 8800 COMPUTER

1980s

NOW

Chapter ‹ 3 ›

Coding Languages

People around the world speak different languages.

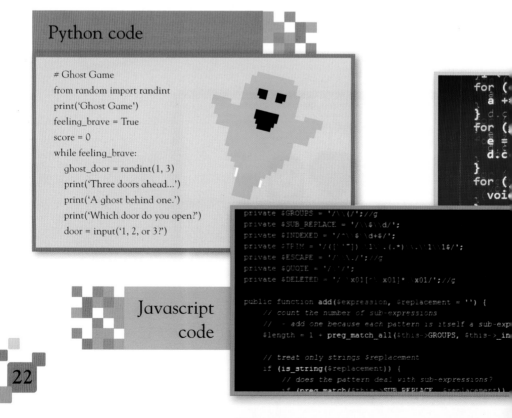

Python code

```
# Ghost Game
from random import randint
print('Ghost Game')
feeling_brave = True
score = 0
while feeling_brave:
    ghost_door = randint(1, 3)
    print('Three doors ahead...')
    print('A ghost behind one.')
    print('Which door do you open?')
    door = input('1, 2, or 3?')
```

```
for (
a +
} d.c
for (
e =
d.c
}
for (
voi
```

```
private $GROUPS = '/\\,(/';//g
private $SUB_REPLACE = '/\\&\\d/';
private $INDEXED = '/\\&\d+&/';
private $TRIM = '/([' '"]) \1\ .(.*) \.\.1 \16/';
private $ESCAPE = '/\\\./';//g
private $QUOTE = '/.'/';
private $DELETED = '/ x01['\ x01]* \x01/';//g

public function add($expression, $replacement = '') {
    // count the number of sub-expressions
    // - add one because each pattern is itself a sub-exp
    $length = 1 + preg_match_all($this->GROUPS, $this->_in

    // treat only strings $replacement
    if (is_string($replacement)) {
        // does the pattern deal with sub-expressions?
        if (preg_match($this->SUB_REPLACE, $replacement)) {
```

Javascript code

Computers have different languages, too. A computer coder needs to use a language that the computer understands.

Basic code

Scratch code

C++ code

One of the simplest coding languages is "binary." Binary is made up of 1s and 0s. Different arrangements of 1s and 0s give the computer different instructions.

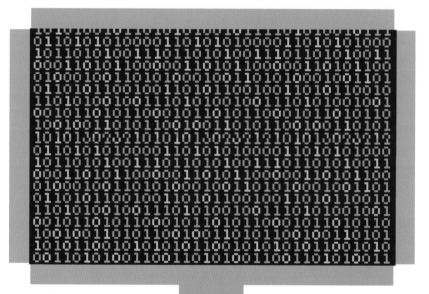

Computers use binary code to send, receive, and store information.

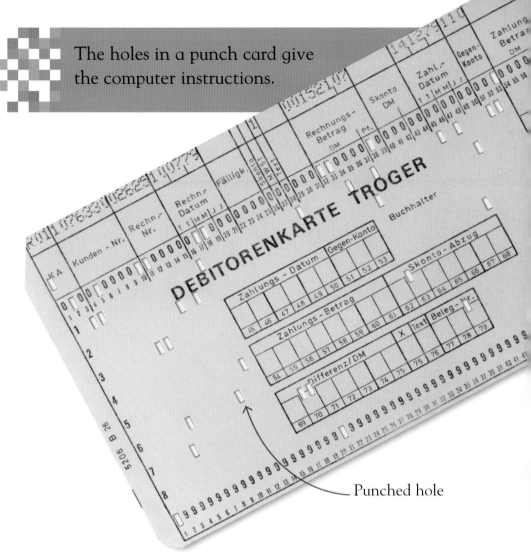

The holes in a punch card give the computer instructions.

Punched hole

Binary code is similar to punch cards with different arrangements of holes. Punch cards were used to **input** coding until the 1970s.

More powerful computers
and better software led to new
coding languages. Coders type
short commands on the keyboard
instead of 1s and 0s.

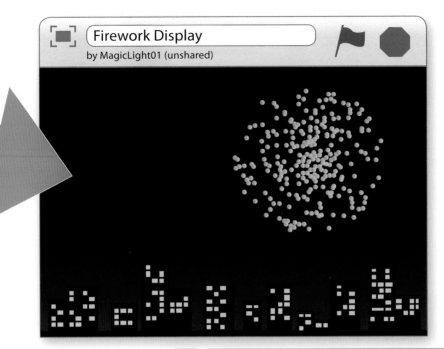

The code on the screen created this firework display.

Over time, most computer languages have become quicker and easier. Now, many pieces of code are **pre-programmed**. Coders click on pieces of code. Then they put the pieces of code together to create a whole new program.

27

Have you noticed that many **website** names begin with "www?" It stands for "World Wide Web."

Computers have been linked by the **Internet** since the 1960s. In 1989, Tim Berners-Lee invented the World Wide Web. People all over the world started sharing information on websites over the Internet. Today, there are millions of websites on the Internet.

Children around the world can learn
fun facts on Internet websites.

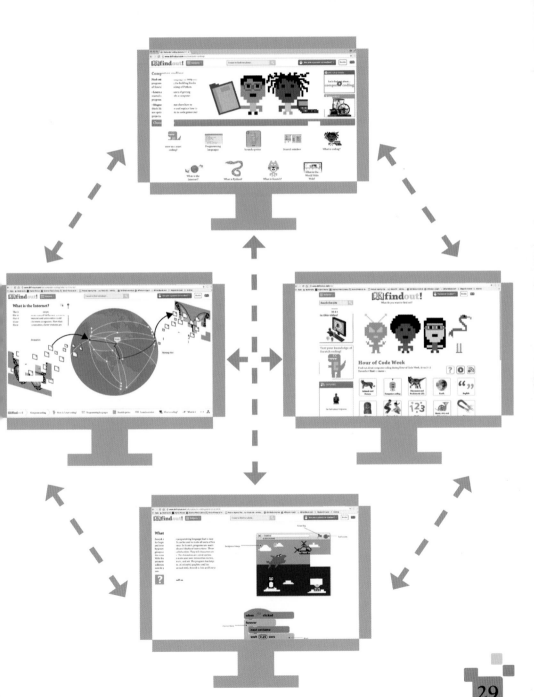

Different Uses

Different coding languages are needed to create codes for different uses. Here are a few.

Coding languages are used to create programs that help children learn.

Coding languages are used to create programs for different types of work.

Coding languages are used to create programs for science labs.

Chapter 4

Coding Today

A modern computer program is called an app. App is short for application.

Apps are easy to **download** onto small computer devices such as cell phones and tablets. With apps, you can carry facts and fun with you all the time!

Many children enjoy using apps just as much as adults do—or maybe even more!

Apps have many different uses. People can play games and music with apps. They can edit photos and videos. Even shopping can be done with apps on the Internet.

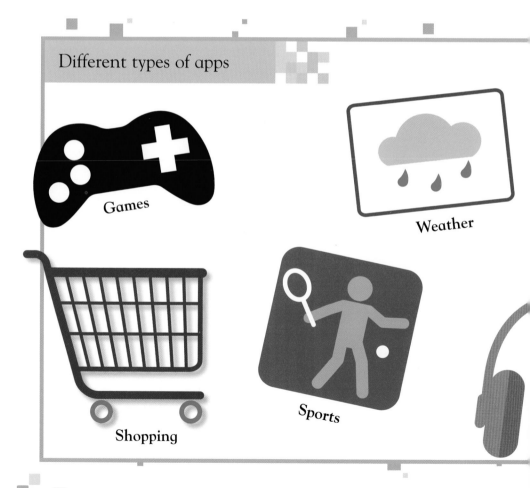

Different types of apps

Games

Weather

Shopping

Sports

People can keep in touch with messaging apps or video calls. They can find out about the weather. There are even apps that help create new apps.

Camera

Messaging

Vacations

Music

Video

All programs need code in order to work. Coding languages, such as Scratch and Python, are easy for everyone to use.

Scratch is perfect for learning how to code.

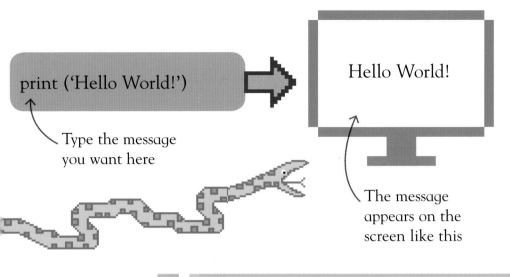

print ('Hello World!')

Type the message you want here

Hello World!

The message appears on the screen like this

Python can be used to create different types of programs.

These days, anyone can code! Anvitha Vijay from Australia was seven years old when she started creating apps. Her apps have had thousands of downloads.

Anvitha Vijay

Coding can be a fun hobby or an interesting job. Many children practice coding at school.

Children in coding club

There are coding clubs and camps, too. One thing is for sure—the ideas for coding are endless!

Scratch Coding

Coders can create games and **animations** with Scratch.

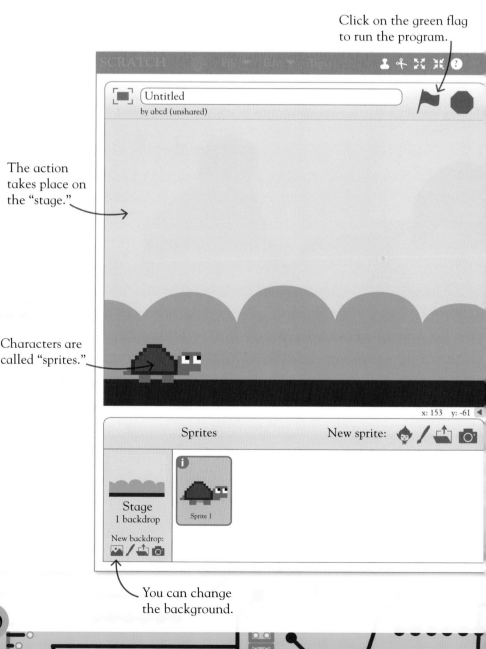

Click on the green flag to run the program.

The action takes place on the "stage."

Characters are called "sprites."

You can change the background.

You can choose different sprites, or create your own!

Instructions for the program are called the "script."

Current sprite with its position on the stage.

Scripts   Costumes   Sounds

Motion
Looks
Sound
Pen
Data

Events
Control
Sensing
Operators
More Blocks

x: -153
y: 61

move (10) steps

turn ↻ (15) degrees

turn ↺ (15) degrees

point in direction (90) ▼

point towards [▼]

go to x: (0) y: (0)

go to [mouse-pointer ▼]

glide (1) secs to x: (0) y: (0)

when 🏳 clicked
forever
   go to [mouse-pointer ▼]
   move (10) steps

This script tells the tortoise on the stage to move 10 steps. The "forever" block repeats the action again and again!

⊖ = ⊕

Backpack

Choose blocks of pre-programmed code for the script.

41

Coding Tips

Learn different coding languages.

Try working as a team and sharing ideas with your friends.

Learn new skills at a coding club, class, or camp.

Experiment! Keep trying and don't be afraid to make mistakes.

Coding Quiz

1. Is the program that tells a computer what to do called "hardware" or "software?"

2. Who is known as the world's first computer programmer?

3. Which early computer language is made up of 1s and 0s?

4. What does "www" stand for at the beginning of a website name?

5. What is the word "app" short for?

Answers on page 45

Glossary

animations
moving images or graphics created by a computer

computer chips
small electronic circuits used in computers

devices
machines used for a particular purpose

download
send a computer file from one computer to another

ENIAC
Electronic Numerical Integrator and Computer

input
put information into a computer

Internet
huge network linking computers around the world

pre-programmed
coded in advance, ready to use

satellites
devices orbiting the Earth, used to send and receive information

tasks
types of work

website
location on the World Wide Web with linked pages

Answers to Coding Quiz:
1. Software; 2. Ada Lovelace;
3. Binary; 4. World Wide Web;
5. Application

Guide for Parents

This book is part of an exciting four-level reading series for children, developing the habit of reading widely for both pleasure and information. These chapter books have a compelling main narrative to suit your child's reading ability. Each book is designed to develop your child's reading skills, fluency, grammar awareness, and comprehension in order to build confidence and engagement when reading.

Ready for a *Level 2* book

YOUR CHILD SHOULD

- be familiar with using beginning letter sounds and context clues to figure out unfamiliar words.
- be aware of the need for a slight pause at commas and a longer one at periods.
- alter his/her expression for questions and exclamations.

A VALUABLE AND SHARED READING EXPERIENCE

For many children, reading requires much effort, but adult participation can make this both fun and easier. So here are a few tips on how to use this book with your child.

TIP 1 Check out the contents together before your child begins:

- read the text about the book on the back cover.
- flip through the book and stop to chat about the contents page together to heighten your child's interest and expectation.
- make use of unfamiliar or difficult words on the page in a brief discussion.
- chat about the nonfiction reading features used in the book, such as headings, captions, or labels.

TIP 2 Support your child as he/she reads the story pages:

- give the book to your child to read and turn the pages.
- where necessary, encourage your child to break a word into syllables, sound out each one, and then flow the syllables together. Ask him/her to reread the sentence to check the meaning.
- you may need to help read some new vocabulary words that are difficult for your child to sound out.
- when there's a question mark or an exclamation point, encourage your child to vary his/her voice as he/she reads the sentence. Demonstrate how to do this if it is helpful.

TIP 3 Chat at the end of each page:

- ask questions about the text and the meaning of the words used. These help to develop comprehension skills and awareness of the language used.

A FEW ADDITIONAL TIPS

- Always encourage your child to try reading difficult words by themselves. Praise any self-corrections, for example, "I like the way you sounded out that word and then changed the way you said it, to make sense."
- Try to read together everyday. Reading little and often is best. These books are divided into manageable chapters for one reading session. However, after 10 minutes, only keep going if your child wants to read on.
- Read other books of different types to your child just for enjoyment and information.

Series consultant, **Dr. Linda Gambrell**, Distinguished Professor of Education at Clemson University, has served as President of the National Reading Conference, the College Reading Association, and the International Reading Association.

Index